The Creation Serie
A Bible-based Read

People

Carole Leah
and Sharon Rentta

NOTE TO PARENTS AND TEACHERS

The Creation Series consists of eight books based on the Genesis account in the Bible. This is the seventh book of this series and has been written from a Christian viewpoint. It is intended to be read *to* 3-4 year olds. The series prepares children to read and extend their vocabulary. In this book children can develop and practise preparatory skills for reading as well as realise God's goodness in creation.

BIBLE REFERENCES

All Bible references are in bold throughout and are as follows: p16: Genesis 1:31, 28.

ENCOURAGE CHILDREN TO:

* Talk about the illustrations and retell the story in their own words.
* Collect pictures of all kinds of people which can be stuck onto card/paper and made into their own book.
* Draw a picture of themselves.
* Memorise the Bible verse and its reference (see page 24).
* Name the different parts of their bodies.
* Look at and talk about the various homes of people who live in their street, village, town or city, e.g. bungalows, flats, huts, houses, tents etc.
* Ensure that the children know the meaning of all these words: *for ever* (always, on and on and on, with no end); *in charge of* (over, to look after, to lead, to care); *ribs* (bones in the top part of our body); *tasty* (very nice in the mouth).

Carole Leah became a Christian at a youth camp when she was seventeen years old while reading a Gideon New Testament. She felt called to write these books so that young children would learn the truth about God while also developing their reading and vocabulary skills. Several people have worked alongside Carole as she wrote this material but she would like to especially dedicate these books to the memory of her dear friend Ruth Martin who gave so much support.

Text copyright © Carole Leah. Illustrations copyright © Sharon Rentta
ISBN: 978-1-84550-535-6 Published by Christian Focus Publications, Geanies House, Fearn, Tain, Ross-shire, IV20 ITW, Scotland, U.K
www.christianfocus.com

Todd, Daniel and Joy are at the market.
See what they are doing in this book!

The children are shopping with a friend.
They are looking at some fruits and vegetables.

Look for the ladybirds!

Can you find pictures of 10 ladybirds in this book?

Did you know that ladybirds go to sleep in the
winter under some wood, on a post or in a shed?

In the beginning

no people lived on the Earth.

God said 'Let us make people.

They will be like us and

they will live for ever.'

First of all, God created a man.

God used soil from the ground to make him.

God breathed into him and

he began to live.

He was called Adam.

God planted a beautiful garden in Eden.

God put Adam in this garden to take

care of it.

God wanted Adam to have

a special friend to help him.

So, God brought all the birds and

animals to him.

Adam named each one of them but

he did not find a special friend to help him.

Then, God did something very wonderful.

First, he helped Adam to sleep very, very deeply.

Then, God created a woman from

one of Adam's ribs.

God brought the woman to Adam.

She became Adam's wife.

Adam called her Eve.

She was Adam's special friend and

they cared for the garden together.

God was good to Adam and Eve.

God gave them tasty seeds, nuts and

fruits to eat.

God put Adam and

Eve in charge of all his world.

So then, they were in charge of

all God's plants and creatures.

God looked at everything he had made and

he was very pleased...

Everything was very good!

God blessed Adam and Eve.

He said, '**...Have many children...**'

God wanted to see people

living all over the Earth.

God wanted people to look after his world.

God loves everyone, everywhere.

He is our Father in heaven.

Every person in the world is special to God.

There is no-one else like Daniel.

There is no-one else like Joy.

There is no-one else like Todd.

Each one is very, very different and

very, very special.

19

God wants Daniel, Joy and

Todd to be like himself.

God wants them to care for other people

like he does.

He wants them to know that

he is their loving Father.

Todd, Joy and Daniel are happy.

God cares for them all the time.

God cares for us all the time, too!

We are all special to God.

Whatever happens, we can know that

God loves us all the time.

Jesus said: '...**even the hairs of your head have all been counted. So do not be afraid...**'

Matthew, chapter 10, verses 30-31